TODAY I CRIED BUT TOMORROW I'LL RISE

*An anthology of poems on rising and overcoming,
written by hearts from all over the world*

www.Holon.co

ISBN#: 978-1-955342-31-5 (Paperback)
ISBN#: 978-1-955342-35-3 (eBook)

Published by:

Holon Publishing & Collective Press
A Storytelling Company
www.Holon.co

CONTENTS

INTRODUCTION

This anthology that you hold in your hands is written from people all over the world… real people with real stories of pain, just like you. They have all come together, writing under the title *Today I Cried, But Tomorrow I'll Rise*, but through their own pain and heart. They are writing in hopes of connecting with you and sharing the moments where they had to choose to rise. Our hope is that you are inspired and encouraged as you read our stories of overcoming.

Another very special part of this anthology is the stories behind the poems, which you will get to read after each poem. This will be an opportunity to hear even more from the author and experience the deeper meaning behind the art. You will connect even more with the writer and better understand their fight to rise.

CHAD RUTTAN

Bitter winds holding me back,
Bleak days feel like they have been black,

      Making me feel like my spirit will break,
Bitter stings from my past,
Deep pain making me lose my way,

      Making me feel like my spirit will break.
Bitter tears drown my voice,
Living life this way, not by choice,

      Making me feel like my spirit will break.

Little things give me hope,
Welcome gifts that will help me cope,

      Making me feel like my spirit will rise.
Little sights of light aloft,
Warmth from the sun that feels soft,

      Making me feel like my spirit will rise.
Little thoughts give me peace,
Memories that love will not let cease,

      Making me feel like my spirit will rise.

Rising sun lights my way,
Resolve to love life each new day,

      Making me feel like my spirit has risen.
Rising joy fills my heart,
Giving me vigor for the new start,

      Making me feel like my spirit has risen.
Rising strength in my soul,
Feeling hope that I can be whole,

      Making me feel like my spirit has risen.

BEHIND THE POEM

My name is Chad. I was born in Edmonton, Alberta, Canada in the early eighties, and spent most of my childhood in the home my parents are still living in. As a child, my ADHD went undiagnosed, which led to many struggles at school and home, including being bullied and misunderstood. I went to college in the Landscape Architecture Technology field, and after working in various jobs in the construction industry, I was employed by a landscape architectural firm. It was a high-stress job, with tight deadlines and a difficult employer. The stress and the time spent at my desk began to make it difficult to sleep and had negative impacts on my physical health.

After 6 years at that firm, I was invited to work for a different company, which came with the stress of a high-pressure environment and additional stress that I placed on myself to perform exceptionally well because I was treated well by my new employer. At age 33, I was finally diagnosed with ADHD after becoming frustrated with my inability to manage my time well and stay on track, which made my job difficult.

Shortly after I was married, I was diagnosed with depression for the first time and suffered my first moderate depressive episode. I was given a month off by my employer, attended therapy regularly, and was able to pull myself out of the episode over six months, for the most part. I never did return to a 5-day work week, and instead worked 4 days a week.

After about two years, my first child was born — a little girl. This life change, along with the stress of my job and my wife's inability to find work, led to us deciding to relocate to my wife's hometown of Rochester, Minnesota. Due to confusion around the immigration process and some less than accurate legal advice, I was turned away at the border and had to say goodbye to my wife and daughter. I spent a year and a half working my way through the process, only able to see my little family every 4 months.

During that wait, I had my first real experience with my anxiety disorder. I convinced myself that I would be turned away again and would not be able to live with my family, which pushed me into another episode of depression. It all worked out in the end, and I was able to rejoin my family in Minnesota, taking on the role of the stay-at-home parent. Looking back now, I can see that I was struggling with the role but managed to do well enough.

Within 10 months of me moving down to the US, my son was born. Shortly after he was born, COVID-19 arrived and shut things down. Throughout that summer, I could see signs that I was beginning to falter — signs that I didn't see right away. That fall, my wife injured her wrists at work, and for a while she had limited use of her hands. At the same time, we sold our house in Canada, then sold our two old cars and bought a new one.

I was unable to visit my family, and they were unable to visit me. All of this stress combined led to a major breakdown in my mental health. At the end of October 2020, I was hospitalized for the first time with severe depression for 8 days. While I was hospitalized, I was diagnosed with generalized anxiety disorder, which had been there, under the surface, for a long time. I was discharged to an outpatient program, which was ended early by a second hospitalization just 3 weeks after being discharged the first time. I was in the hospital for another 8 days, spent the weekend at home, and then checked into a residential depression treatment program in Wisconsin.

10 days after my arrival at the facility, I was exposed to COVID-19. I was temporarily discharged to quarantine at a local hotel for 10 days. I lasted a day and a half before I needed to be hospitalized again, this time at the inpatient ward on the grounds of the treatment facility. I was quarantined in my room for 6 days, which were some of the darkest days of my life. My last two days of inpatient were spent out of quarantine. While waiting for the residence to reopen, I celebrated Christmas with my fellow patients, and I even received a donated gift. I returned to the residence for a further 3 weeks of treatment before being discharged home, which was early because my roommate's snoring kept me awake. I needed another 2 or 3 weeks of treatment, but returning home was the best option I had.

When I got home, my in-laws helped look after the kids. By mid-May, I had taken on more childcare duties, which were going moderately well, until some miscommunication happened around a day that my in-laws were going to be away (I didn't find out until they didn't show up). This led to my worst breakdown yet. I was hospitalized again, this time for 12 days, during which I came down with a nasty case of diverticulitis, which is an infection in the colon. Once I was well enough, I was discharged home. With the exception of one overnight stay in the ER, I have been doing much better. I found a used charcoal grill, which I enjoy using immensely, and have taught myself how to bake. I have exercised my creativity in the kitchen as well as in painting and writing. I still have to be very cautious to not become overwhelmed, but I am making good progress every day.

ABOUT CHAD

Chad is a middle-aged father of two young children and a husband to a beautiful wife. He enjoys cooking, baking, reading, writing, painting, woodworking, hiking, and mountain biking. Time spent in nature is when he feels the most at peace. He has traveled to many different countries and wants to visit more. Chad was born in Canada but now lives in Rochester, Minnesota.

LOURIN KHALAF

In the space within my mind
Lies a box uniquely designed

A box filled with hellos and goodbyes
And people I hold dear in my eyes

A box filled with thoughts that run for miles
And the paint brushes that drew my smiles

In it lie the piano keys that moved my heart
And music pieces that mended its wounded parts

Others have boxes too
Filled with stories and many truths

Their boxes glimmer in purples and blues
In different shapes and many warm hues

As beautiful as jewels
All uniquely designed.

BEHIND THE POEM

I write this poem to appreciate how uniquely designed we are as human beings. Every so often, I catch myself falling into a cycle of comparison. I compare myself to another person and ultimately feel discouraged. I forget about my own strengths and end up focusing on my shortcomings. I write this poem to remind myself and many others that being unique is our strong suit. Realizing that we don't excel in something allows us to appreciate those who do. Moreover, sometimes recognizing people's talents is our talent. For instance, an art critic's talent lies in their love for art. They didn't necessarily create the artwork, but that's why they can admire the artist who created something that they did not. Consequently, I use "boxes" to symbolize our own experiences and individuality. I imagine that these boxes would carry the people we love; shaped by the truths and wisdom we gain during our journey in life. I start by mentioning "hellos and goodbyes" as something I would find in my box because in life we greet and meet many people. The first people we meet are our parents — two people who decided to give us pieces of themselves. We then make friends with people who we once identified as strangers. Some friends open wounds, and some others help us mend them.

Ultimately, every hello ends with a goodbye, and there are goodbyes that we say and some which we only receive. I incorporate elements that represent the things

I love, which I expect to find in my box. I used paint brushes to refer to art, which has been a big part of my teenage years. Art has brought me so much joy and excitement, especially painting. Piano keys symbolized music, which I confide in whenever I am feeling upset. I go on to describe other people's boxes. I use color and shapes to recognize the individuality and uniqueness of each person. In my last two verses, I compare people to jewels because while every gemstone is different, it is still shines.

Their words were foreign to my ears
The environment was different, which only fed my fears
I feared standing out from many
I didn't have one reason to, I had plenty

My mother tongue was of different colours
My food smelt like home to me, but not to others
I often felt misunderstood
My words didn't reach them like I thought they would

Where I come from our history is deep
Our ancestors were Pharaohs and proud Queens
They spoke languages we currently cannot speak,
And left behind secrets we are unable to reveal
The pyramids remain a world mystery
Where many scholars study history

It was challenging to embrace my golden roots
Instead of deeming them as troublesome attributes
So, if I can't help but shape your words into sounds
that I can speak
Don't belittle me, for my accent isn't all there is to me.

BEHIND THE POEM

I write this poem to highlight one of many struggles that immigrant families face, the language barrier. Some immigrants might be able to adapt and learn the language, but often many will still have an accent when speaking English. After all, it is hard for an adult to completely change their pronunciation when they have been speaking their mother's tongue for decades. When I was 11 years old, my family moved to Canada, like many others, to seek more opportunities and a better lifestyle. While it might have been easier for my sisters and I to learn the language due to our young age, my parents continue to carry an accent in their speech. The same language can sound slightly different coming from people of diverse backgrounds and ethnic groups. I think that's beautiful. The words we speak are a reflection of who we are now and who we were in the past. Essentially, wouldn't it be too boring if everyone had the same exact story?

Unfortunately, there are many people who do not share the same opinion as me when it comes to accents. Accents are often associated with ignorance, lack of intelligence, and many other negative associations. The fact that immigrant families come from backgrounds of respected and cultivating cultures is often overlooked. I am of Coptic Egyptian ethnicity, hence in my poem I refer to Egypt's rich history. When I was younger, I heard amazing stories about many Egyptian artifacts.

Many of which include the solar alignment of King Ramses' statue. Twice a year, King Ramses' statue is bathed in the golden sunrays to honor his birthdate and his coronation day. While ancient Egyptians did not have the technology we have today, they were still able to gain knowledge of the stars and fully understand our solar system. My knowledge may be limited to my Egyptian background but imagine how many more astonishing artifacts exist within other cultures. Furthermore, every artifact carries a connection to a lineage much wiser than we are. It is incredibly hard to believe that people who came from such deep backgrounds lack intelligence.

ABOUT LOURIN

Lourin Khalaf lives in Canada. She is a medical student at St. George University, who has always enjoyed writing poetry. In her free time, she enjoys painting, writing, and going out for walks. In her teenage years, she explored illustrative painting and illustrated folktales from many different cultures. Her artwork often incorporated a variety of beautiful landscapes, which conveyed her love for nature. In her literary work, Lourin advocates for mental health, self-love, and body positivity. She also touches upon some social issues such as gender inequality. Her love for nature is manifested as a recurrent theme in many of her poems.

Through writing, Lourin wishes to connect and emphasize with the readers. She hopes to empower them and remind them that they are not alone.

DEANNE PERSINGER

There is no joy in heartbreak,
No happiness in hurt,
No satisfaction in loss,
No serenity in sorrow,
No contentment in failure,
No bliss in misery,
No delight in struggle,
No rejoicing in adversity,
No peace in suffering,
No gladness in anguish,
No comfort in woe,
No jubilation in defeat;
However,
There is hope in possibility,
Strength in determination,
Advantage in intention,
Courage in climbing mountains,
Fortitude in resilience,
Confidence in clearing hurdles,
Fulfillment in diligence,
Gratification in overcoming,
Power in tenacity,
Moxie in conquering,
Grit in dedication,
Achievement in perseverance,
Grace from God,
And blessings to be discovered.

BEHIND THE POEM

A couple of years ago, my heart broke for my daughter. If you have children that participate in travel sports, you will understand our pain. I have often said that soccer tryouts are the worst time of the year, and that particular year was torturous for us. My son got an offer for the same team that he had been on the previous year on the very first day of tryouts. He was happy, and thus, we were happy. However, my daughter's story was not so delightful. She didn't get an offer on the first night. The next 24 hours were filled with anxiety, leading up to the second day of tryouts and waiting for an offer. I was nauseous. I barely slept. I tried my best not to let my nerves show so I didn't make my girl more anxious. My husband and I encouraged her to do her best on day two and told her we were proud of her, no matter what. When the offer finally came, it was not with her current teammates/friends. She was also made aware from the team text string that everyone else had received offers to remain on the same team, and she was the only one left off of that new team. So incredibly hard!

Many tears fell that day from my daughter and from me. No parent wants to see their child disappointed and hurting. I wrote this poem to let my daughter know that life doesn't feel fair sometimes, and it was okay to walk through all of the emotions she was feeling. I knew she felt crushed. I didn't want her stuck in a negative mindset, but rather to move forward and grow from the experience. I wanted it to be a time for her to figure out if this would make her work harder and get back on her old team, be content with her current team, or decide to focus on another sport or pastime. I prayed hard for her during this time. I prayed that she has more hills than valleys in her life, like the one she was walking through. I also prayed that she would learn, grow, rise, and gain strength and perspective when she faces troubles.

After this difficult time, my daughter figured out what she wanted and worked extra hard to reach her goal. I am so proud of her determination and dedication! She is now back on the team with her friends. Even though this poem was originally written about not making a soccer team, it can translate to all types of disappointments and adversity.

Disbelieving wails bellow from deep within.
My eyes continually overflow with grief.
Shredded expectations, demolished dreams,
Darkness overtakes, how can I go on?
Trembling, denying, shrieking, dying,
Dying the death of reality without you.
Longing for one more day, one more conversation,
Sorrow sinks my body, my legs give way.
In great lament, my pleas to God fill the room.
Weeping, regretting, hurting, howling,
Stunned and immobilized in my loss,
Abundant cries of heartache ring out.
There's a vast expanse from your missing presence.
I pray with my entire being, "God hold me!"
Commemorating, speaking, memorizing, reflecting,
Sadness gives way to gratitude for time shared.
Relinquishing the what-ifs, clinging to what was,
Loving you means finding joy in what is.
You would want nothing less for me.
Celebrating, adoring, honoring, exalting,
The Holy Spirit gives me strength and peace.
The richness of memories engulf my heart,
Recollection illuminates the good
As I cherish the blessings of then and now.
Remembering, loving, transforming, rising.

BEHIND THE POEM

My father-in-law, George, was diagnosed with small cell lung cancer with metastasis to his spine and some other areas. It was a fast-growing cancer with a poor prognosis. Even though that was the case, I remained hopeful that he would live a lot longer so he could watch my kids and his other grandchildren grow up.

When George finished radiation, he ended up with pneumonia. After being treated for that, chemotherapy was started. He tolerated the treatments well for a few days, but then he deteriorated. At the end of the month, he had a quick decline. My husband packed up and drove the 600 miles to be with his parents. I was so thankful that he got there in time to say goodbye.

At the same time, I was home alone with my kids, who were ages 12 and 9. It was devastatingly painful trying to navigate the emotions of losing my beloved father-in-law and my kids' sadness in losing their grandfather after only four months of being sick. My kids decided to go to school that week after hearing the news because the memorial for George wasn't going to be for another month. My husband remained with his mom that week, which I am grateful he could do, but mourning without my best friend was nearly more than I could handle.

As the weeks and months passed, we talked about him and celebrated his life. I was comforted in knowing he was in a better place, in the gratitude of the time we did have together, and in the fond memories we shared.

ABOUT DEANNE

Deanne Persinger is a part-time caseworker serving the aged and disabled in the Indianapolis area, while being a mom and writer. Hope is the most valuable resource she gives to her clients and readers. She and her husband, Charles, have two nearly-grown children, the best dog in the world, and a cat that the dog pesters.

Deanne has completed her first book and is looking for a publisher. This debut book is a Christian non-fiction collection of true inspirational stories aimed at helping readers find blessings in adversity. If you want to be one of the first to find out when her book will come out, subscribe to her website at deannepersinger. com. You can also find her on Instagram and Facebook @deannepersingerwrites and on her blog at deannepersinger.wordpress.com.

NICCI JO BROSE

I am a warrior, but today I could not stand.
My heart sucked into the depths of life's sinking sand.

The fear of the future gripped me so tight.
It destroyed my hope and took away my fight.

Paralyzed by my thoughts that continued to race.
Consumed by the reality of what I could face.

What will be stripped of me and what will remain?
Then God softly reminded me, "There is still so much to gain."

So today I cried, but tomorrow I'll rise.
Mind renewed and rebuking the lies.

I am still a warrior even when I can not stand.
God has given me "Aarons" to hold up my hand.

I feel my army carrying me through these nights.
Fear is fading as my hope reignites.

I've taken captive my thoughts and given myself grace.
Accepting that I'll have these moments throughout my race.

But remembering to always surrender my life and my pain.
Knowing that God will 50:20 it all and the world will gain.

So today I cried, but tomorrow I'll rise.
Giving Him glory through the joy and the cries.

BEHIND THE POEM

This was the very first "Today I Cried, but Tomorrow I'll Rise" poem. It came out of such a painful place, as I was dealing with my first really bad MS flare up after being diagnosed with this new lifestyle. I felt so positive and strong when the doctor called me on November 11th 2019. I was full of hope and so ready to take on this new journey. BUT then the reality of what I was facing hit me like a ton of bricks.

As I struggled to accept what was happening and trying to process what I was feeling, I picked up the pen and began to let the pain pour into the paper. Midway through the writing, I felt a flip in my spirit… a peace… a strength… a "It is going to be ok, Nicci, for tomorrow you will rise."

This poem became my anthem as I learned to embrace the struggle and allow myself to have those moments and rough days. It is ok to have those moments… we just can't remain in them. I have always thought I had to be strong all the time. God has taught me and reminded me through my MS journey that it is ok to have those "today I cried" moments. I must give myself grace in those moments and rise tomorrow, knowing and trusting that He will use all my tears of today to water the beauty of my tomorrows. Whatever daily battle you are facing, I pray that you are able to embrace the journey, give yourself grace on those tough days, and then rise like the warrior you were created to be.

A part of life that my heart has grown to hate
Are the moments my loved ones enter heaven's gate.
All the said goodbyes ripping through my heart
Wondering if the pain last forever...no end to this start
The start of life that misses someone every single day
Yearning for a touch, a smell, or hearing words they say
But the words are no more and the smells slowly fade away

So today I cried, but tomorrow I'll rise

I will learn to celebrate the amazing life that they walked.
And rejoice that for them doors of heaven have been
    unlocked.
I will learn to continue my journey that lies ahead
Instead of living as if I too am already dead
For they would not want me to stop living just because
    they are no longer here
They would want me to dream big, live bold, and walk
    with no fear
They would say, "Nicci Jo, make me proud...make the
    heavens cheer."

So today I cried, but tomorrow I'll rise.
Making praises from all my cries.

BEHIND THE POEM

Death is difficult for everyone... it sucks. We can't avoid it, and it shatters our hearts every time we have to say goodbye to someone we love so deeply. We all have different ways of coping when this happens. For me, I just didn't cope. I would not acknowledge their previous existence... could not and would not look at pictures and would never just sit and enjoy a walk down memory lane. If I saw them in a picture or talked about them, then they become real again, and the reality of them being gone was a truth I had to face. So, my brain would just try to wipe them from my memories, and forget that they ever walked on this earth.

This was so hurtful for those around me who coped differently than me. Those who needed to talk and share memories couldn't do so around me. After my Grandma Jo lost her husband... my sweet Grandpa... she would always try to talk to me about my inability to cope. She would tell me with tears running down her face how worried she was about me. She would tell me how hurtful it was to just erase him and others from life, and that I was not only hurting those around me but also hurting myself. She would always give me talks about how healing it would be to just allow myself to feel and be sad... to really walk through the mourning process. I listened to her... I apologized and held her as she cried. BUT my heart just couldn't. It was so hard and couldn't handle the pain of allowing it to soften and feel the grief.

I did this through so many deaths, and Grandma Jo would give me the talk each time. But then she got sick. So much I could go into in those five words you just read. Through this time of her fighting many different things for several years, she would continue to have these discussions with me. Then at one point, we all thought the end was near, and she sat me down and asked me to do her funeral. What?! Seriously?! I don't do death, period, and you want me to actually do your funeral service?! But I smiled and agreed and listened as she told me some things she would like done. But that warrior pulled through, and it wasn't her time. She was still sick and battling, but she was still here.

Then my little family moved out of state and was now two and a half hours away. We came back when we could to see family, but it wasn't a lot. I'll never forget the call... the moment they knew the time was very near. She was surrounded by family but was holding on. I was trying to plan when and how I was going to get there, and then my cousin called and told me that she felt Grandma was waiting on me and wanted me there. I dropped everything and left, getting there as fast as I could.

It was late when I got there, but it felt so good seeing family in that moment. We all were circled around her as it grew later and later into the night. People began to leave, but I felt this strong urge to stay with her. Everyone eventually left. It was just Grandma Jo, myself, and a picture of Grandpa on the wall of her room. I sat next to her, holding her hand, watching the life literally leave her body. I talked to her. I cried. I felt. It was not long at all… maybe an hour or so of sitting with her, just her and me, when she took that final breath. A supernatural peace filled the room as her spirit left her body. I sat in that peace, imagining her with my sweet Grandpa once again. I sat, holding her hand as the warmth slowly left her body, but I still felt that peace when thinking of the cherished memories, the wisdom she shared, and the love she always made me feel. In that moment of her passing, I was already learning the lessons of mourning she had tried to teach me for so many years.

Yes, I did the funeral like she asked me to. I felt so much strength and peace from the moment she passed and through planning and doing the funeral service. It is so funny that the message that God gave me to share at her funeral was the very thing I needed to hear and do myself. It was about learning to embrace the onward passing… the physical passing on of their spirit BUT focusing on the downward passing… the life, lessons, and legacy that they passed down to us. I was so blessed to have my Grandma Jo and all the wisdom and love she gave and passed down to me. I gained so much from her life, but the greatest lesson she taught me was how to lose her.

ABOUT NICCI JO

Sharing my writing with the world... it's something I never thought I would do. But then God taught me that all those things He puts on my heart are not just for me, but for the hearts of the world. So here I am, writing from my heart to yours.

Beyond writing, I have a hubby of almost 18 years and three beautiful girls! Two of them are still those weird alien teenagers that we feed and try to understand on the daily, while the oldest is happily married with two sweet little boys. My favorite thing to do besides writing is be with my family. I love to watch my girls compete in MMA and wrestling, sing in choir concerts, and whatever else brings joy to their hearts. I love to cuddle with them and watch ridiculous romcoms and hallmark movies that are so predictable, but we still sit and cry. Love my family time!

I am also an ordained pastor and love to circle up and do life with women. I have a women's ministry that just began this year called "Women Beyond the Walls." There is nothing like a group of women, from all walks of life, churches, backgrounds, cultures, generations... all of their differences coming together to grow and encourage one another.

I not only find joy in teaching women, but also my little 2nd graders. I am an elementary teacher and have been blessed to wear the teacher hat for over a decade now.

I can't go without mentioning that we have two fur babies! Nina, our little chihuahua, who is so old and the biggest lap dog ever. AND the 2-year-old Aussie, Wendy, who annoys the world out of Nina and us, but also who we love so dearly!

I pray that every time you read something from my heart, that your heart is inspired, warmed, and forever changed. Happy reading! :)

PETRO
MBWANYA

I tried, I tried, and failed
I tried, tried, I lost
I tried, and tried,
I failed, and failed
So disappointed I felt
So depressed I was
Bitterness feeding my heart
Tears filling my eyes
Falling down my cheeks
Tears not of joy
But those of defeat
Telling myself this is it
I can no longer stand and compete
For I have tried, tried, and tried
But instead of savoring success
I cried, cried, and cried
For to the feast of those victorious
I had no access, no place
I wasn't invited, no cries allowed
Yes, I cried aloud

And as I reached the climax of pain
I felt I was only crying in vain
I couldn't cry no more
I stopped it there
For I felt there was another person next to me
Who also wept with me
But I felt He wasn't only crying with me

He was also crying for me
He cried because of me
He cried because I cried
He cried because He didn't want me to cry
He cried because He cared
He made my cries his
My mourns his own

Amazed I was
Ablaze with joy
Relieved I felt
Renewed was my joy
Overjoyed is what I was
When He said to me
Cry no more my child
The future I've forged for you is bright
The words literally dried my tears in a rush
Then He adds, today you tried, failed, and cried
Tomorrow you shall rise, fight, and win a crown

BEHIND THE POEM

My moment of depression was one of the darkest seasons of my life. It all started when I moved from my country to South Africa. It was the impact of the relocation, the struggle to acclimatize with the new environment, and, most severely, a prolonged period of almost absolute loneliness. But besides these factors, my dark age was also nourished by a number of unfortunate events that occurred back home after I had left. One of those was my father falling ill and not being able to stand on his feet for about a year and half. This event in particular was of a remarkably devastating contribution, and it had an especially terrible repercussion on my life this side of South Africa, and nothing we had planned as a family could happen as intended. So, I gradually became a bitter young person — a very hopeless and lonely person. I had lost this vital substance called hope. It had fled far from me. I stopped trusting that things were going to be okay. It was a really horrendous situation to find myself in.

Through that trial, I made a quite intriguing and critical discovery about depression. I learned that depression, like other silent killers, operates and develops so silently and quickly that one never realizes they are in such an unhealthy state until they come or begin to come out of it. And people around might not always notice one is actually internally struggling if they are not observant enough or if they are too busy with their own struggles and completely oblivious to others'. This is, in my opinion, just the scariest part of it — you're battling against a disguised sickness that neither you nor your entourage knows about.

But how did I, Petro, escape this dangerous trap? I became more attentive to the inner me and the little voice of Christ within me, to hear it a little louder, to understand what exactly was not going well and how to overcome it. Because you can only fight and beat an enemy if you know them well, right? So to get some clarity, without which it was impossible to overcome my disease, I learned to value happiness, and I became more intentional about keeping myself happy, having a constant positive mindset, and doing things that brought me joy. Things that I called beautiful. Yes, I learned to see beauty in life, see the smallest joyful things in life and maximize on their precious benefits. Happiness, indeed, provides a clear mind and soul.

So, I became enslaved to the idea of freedom. And true and complete freedom, for me, goes hand-in-hand with unconditional happiness. Learning to be happy for absolutely no apparent reason. Freedom is crazy and wild. You have to go wild with it. And freedom also comes with learning to freely and fearlessly express your most profound thoughts.

Besides making the most out of the least precious elements of our seemingly gloomy life, I also learned to externalize my pain, hurts, worries, and fears. I learned that pain that is let out loses the potential to bite. It becomes weak and harmless like a wet dog. It doesn't matter which way you choose to let out your pain, the result is always effective and impressive.

It was this valuable revelation that taught me to speak to myself, as I was a lonely and taciturn person. This must sound so crazy, I know, but it greatly helped me. Speaking to myself and hearing what my own mouth says to my ears is just the same as attentively, internally listening to my heart. This is an interestingly important part of the thinking process for me. Why? Because sometimes one does not clearly make sense of thoughts that travel through their mind unless they can verbalize them. It is the case for me. And this is just one considerable reason why I fondly fell in love with writing — writing poetry in particular. It is such a therapeutic activity. It literally heals my heart with not much effort at all. All I need is to write all my worries down and realize how meaningless they are. And there is a gratifying part of it that also contributes to the healing process. It is the fact that everything in art is admirable. So when you write a piece of poetry, you make art, which not everybody is gifted to do. So you feel a huge sense of achievement. You feel like a small creator. And the feeling, believe me, is absolutely fulfilling.

So this is what I want you to always remember. Remember all the time that clarity does matter if your well-being matters to you. And happiness is a safe state of mind that must always stay with you. It matters more than anything in life. And true happiness comes with a deep sense of freedom. A strong and unshakable conviction that to be fully free is to be fully happy, even when there is visibly nothing to be happy about. Create your own world, and in it, instate your own kind of happiness with the simplest elements and materials of our troubled lives. This is how you rise above your trials. This is how you rise from ashes. This is how you overcome.

ABOUT PETRO

I'm Petro Mbwanya Wabwana, an African, self-taught poet, from the Congo, and author of *My First Mosaic* (https://www.amazon.com/dp/B097YY523Q). A word weaver of an enthusiastically altruistic tendency, a passionate Pan-Africanist, and a global citizen who loves people, cultures, and languages — diversity as a lifestyle. I'm a firm believer in the religion of sharing and caring, an activist for human rights, advocate for less privileged people, a fighter for the humanitarian cause, a lover of God, and an amplifier of the voice of the people — the youth in particular. My entire life and art is purposed for humanity and my philosophy of what it means to be human — to be kind and care for humankind. I'm founding member of Voice1Africa, a young continent-wide Pan-African youth movement (https://www.youtube.com/channel/UCECF2SsQesGWqx-CKnCq3EYw).

SHARON
HURLEY HALL

Today I ripped up your letters
Dissected the words
Tore up the half-truths
Shredded the lies
I once believed.

Today I erased your tapes.
Though I can still hear your voice
Playing in my head
The volume is on low.

Today I looked at you
And saw just a man.
I changed the combination
To my heart.

Today I changed my life.

ABOUT SHARON

Sharon Hurley Hall is an anti-racism activist, writer, and educator. Firmly committed to doing her part to eliminate racism, she is the Founder and Curator-in-Chief of Sharon's Anti-Racism Newsletter (https://www.anti-racismnewsletter.com). Sharon is the author of *Exploring Shadeism*, an analysis of colorism in Barbados and the wider Caribbean. She has won three Bronze awards for poetry in Barbados' NIFCA Literary Arts competition.

PINAL MEHTA

I was silently suffering through many pains,
Sorrow and pain was all in my veins,
I still pretended to be happy in all the ways

Beneath the tree I sat and cried like hell,
All I wanted was to go to the mountains and yell,
But nobody noticed, I wasn't well!

Days, weeks and months passed,
But I was still searching for a ray of sunlight to fill my
dark room with
happiness,
ALAS!

After two months of sorrow and pain,
I finally decided to move on and convince my brain,
After the long journey of sorrow and pain, I decided to
rise again!

That night I cried like hell, but it was for the last time, yeah,
Gradually I convinced my heart by saying,
"Today I cried but tomorrow I'll rise!"

BEHIND THE POEM

'Today I cried, tomorrow I'll rise' poetry is very close to my heart, as it highlights my real efforts and struggles in my darkest times. Hard times are a part of our lives, and all of us have to deal with it. The hardest part of our lives is when someone very dear to us or very close to us leaves us. Death of someone very close to us affects a lot. My story is based on the same. Someone very close to my heart said their final goodbyes to us earlier this year. I was not in a good state of mind, as I never expected them to leave me so soon. I suffered from panic attacks twice or thrice maybe. I was so affected that no matter how much I tried, I couldn't distract myself from their absence.

And the worst part was that I wasn't there with them when they took their last breath. Although I met them a week before they bid their final farewell. But it was hard to believe that someone you loved so much, someone you danced with, partied with, someone you planned outings with, was no longer a part of your life.

But we are talking about my journey of moving on! So, it was way too hard to move on from something like this. I listened to their audio messages on loop for a week or more. Memories hit hard when death occurs. Sometimes all you want to do is escape from reality, but you can't. After a week or two, I realized that it was important to move on with life. One can't sit and stick to one bad chapter of life and keep grieving on it for the rest of their life. Life goes on, so moving on from the bad chapters of life and waiting for the good ones is the best option.

I feel that when you are not in a proper mental health, you need to give yourself some time. Everyone needs some time to escape from the harsh reality of life and find some peace. Giving yourself some time is the best way to move on. Do not be hard on yourself. Everything takes time. Moving on is a slow process; it takes time, but eventually you will. Hard times do not last forever; eventually we all have to move on with life. I still miss them, and I think I will always will, but that doesn't mean that I will sit and cry for my whole life. I realized that I will have to move on with life.

So, I decided to start fresh, try my best to be strong, and face the harsh reality. I think a ray of sunlight is all we need during the darkest parts of life. It's difficult to face the reality and develop the 'never give up' attitude, but it is the right way. Don't give up on yourself or your life. Remember that dark times are a part of life, every scary night follows a beautiful morning. Remember that you are precious, and your life is precious. And no matter what the situation is, life goes on, so eventually we need to rise and shine all over again. Don't let pain and sorrow consume you. Believe in yourself, and believe that all of us have immense strength and power within ourselves. Just identify that power and rise all over gain. Let go of all the pain and grief.

At last, all I would say is that I am grateful to share this part of my life with you, and I am glad to connect with you so personally and whole heartedly.

ABOUT PINAL

Hi, this is Pinal Mehta, a passionate 18-year-old writer who believes in spreading love, peace, and happiness. I hope my poetry, as well as my story behind the poem, motivates and encourages you guys.

Love,
Pinal ♥

RATI BANGA

Today I cried for all moments lost,
For all the tears I shed,
Reminiscing our laughs
And play
Today I cried for silently suffering,
Paining over my wounds
Regretting unsaid words
And trusting you blindly.
But tomorrow I'll rise,
I will let the sunlight heal me
And embrace the war wholeheartedly
I will fight with my all
Love truly and harder
I will make it through each day
Remembering our good moments
Forgiving you for breaking me completely
And come back stronger,
Tomorrow, for more...

BEHIND THE POEM

The story behind this poem is one of a craving for affection, abandonment, and deception from a loved one. For many years, I felt that it was my fault that I wasn't loved or accepted for who I was by someone who was my entire world and the reason for my existence, but I then realised with time that it was never me; the person who should've loved and protected me was too selfish. He chose himself over his children.

I wrote this poem to let go and free myself from the hurt and pain, but alos to treasure the few happy memories we held together. I learnt to love, accept, and give my all to my loved ones. The trauma of my past shouldn't affect my present. I learnt to be a better parent to my children so they never go through what I went through with mine. I have learnt to forgive the ones who broke me and embrace my current family wholeheartedly. They love me like their own, and I am grateful for the love and support I receive from them.

Today I cried,
Not because of sadness
But from for freeing myself,
From the chains
That kept bringing me down
And suffocating my thoughts,
I cried for the small steps I took
Towards success and healing,
For overcoming my pain and suffering
And for feeling my heart beat for the very first time in
a long while
Today I felt,
That my prayers were heard
And the almighty healed my soul
He took in his comforting arms,
To make me whole, fix me piece by piece
And awakened my faith once again.
Tomorrow I'll rise,
To my fullest self form
Start from the beginning
Mark my journey,
Leave my imprints,
Make new memories,
And conquer
The world,
Face the demons that surround within me
Without any fear…

BEHIND THE POEM

The story behind this poem is of reawakening, rebirth, and facing my demons.

I was diagnosed with CRPS (complex regional pain syndrome) at the age of 27. The condition took everything away from my life at the time. I had to learn to live with it, adjust my lifestyle, and accept it. It was a major transformation — no days were the same. I was blessed to have my loved ones and family around, but often I have to battle through it alone. There's no cure. I developed many secondary conditions post this one, and it is difficult to understand what to do and how to cope, but I never left the will to live. The faith stayed within me. I was reborn once again and count my blessings daily for waking up and seeing a new day each morning. I thank God for giving me the courage to get through the tough days and many procedures to keep my body functioning.

Long term illnesses that are invisible can become very challenging to live with, but it's not impossible. There's always a ray of light at the end of a storm, so keep chasing the light — that's what my belief is. I meditate and pray to rise above the pain and suffering.

ABOUT RATI

Rati Banga, aged 36 and also known as Love is Life by Rati, is a published writer, photographer, and artist from Melbourne, Australia. Rati was born in France and loves travelling. She is a warrior who suffers from long-term chronic illness but believes in living and enjoying life fully. Rati writes to let her creative flair, thoughts, dreams, imagination, and emotions all out in a safe place. She is married and has 2 children aged 12 and 6 years old.

Rati has been part of anthologies and has had her work published in several books.

Facebook: Love is Life by Rati

Instagram: @Love.is.life.by.Rati

SAMANTHA JAMES

Too many people playing the victim
That's a flaw in our system
Too many people living in the kingdom
Forgot the people they came from
Too many people craving for freedom
But forgetting not all are welcome
Judging my orientation
While you use violence instead of conversation
Shaming the ethnicity while stealing the culture
Oblivious to the truth but never to the color
Too blinded by the blackness of my complexion
To ever take a look within your own reflexion
Scared of diversity and undesired change
So you observe quietly you enable my pain
Demanding justice within the corruption
Their actions defended, accepted and normalized
But how do you demand justice
when they can't even look you in the eyes
But how do you demand things to change
In a world that has put you in shackles and chains
That has pushed you down and has set you to flames
That shuts you up and refuses to call out your name
How do you beat a game when the rules are bias
And the mentality spreads like a virus
So today I cried but tomorrow ill rise
Ill make you see me and open your eyes
I'm taking these false guidance
To build on my self reliance

Take all this hate you're supplying
Finally release it and put it in writing
We're searching for a freedom we may never gain
The freedom to laugh, to love, to hurt, to get through
   the pain
We're searching for a power we may never obtain
To run, to live, to not be contained
To love who we choose without restrictions
To live a life lacking conditions
Outside the norms, complete liberation
Choose who to be, no definition
Without the rules of gender or race
Is how I wish we were raised
With the acceptance of making mistakes
And to never experience the feeling of being misplaced
To finally be able to remove this mask
This to you is all we ask
To put an end to this rival
Without adding to the cycle

BEHIND THE POEM

My poetry, like much of my writing, doesn't come to life because of specific events that I have had to endure. It's the collaboration of many elements. The emotions I feel and the questions that wander into my head when I'm experiencing extreme sadness, pain, and loss. Writing during these low periods in my life is what I can honestly say saved my life when no one else could. My poems tell the story of pain, fear, anger, perseverance, and triumph. Created throughout the stages of my life when I needed to create my own hope to overcome the darkness that kept me caged in my own head. Writing has become the lifeline I wasn't aware I was in desperate need of. Writing gave me the words for the emotions that I was feeling that my heart couldn't voice.

My poem, like many others, was brought to light through pain. A pain indiscernible to those who've never felt it. A manic pain that comes in waves and never truly leaves as you feel it constantly lurking, never out of reach, always waiting for the opportunity. Pain that comes from devaluing yourself and questioning your own worth. This pain of mine has found ways to manifest itself through my personal battles against depression and anxiety. A pain you feel that spreads through every inch of your body, a pain that drowns your soul and clouds your judgment. A pain that'd make your body shake and that would make your mind break. From feeling so alone every-time I retired to a place called home. By being surrounded by love and support but always feeling like you fall short. For always doubting my abilities and second guessing my worth never feeling adequate. It's the pain that came from never giving up on myself when it seemed everyone else had. It's the pain that came from looking at myself in the mirror when I was broken and at my lowest and had to pick myself up and dry my own tears. But through this pain, I found incredible strength. I found the strength to talk myself off that ledge to try another day. I found a strength that gave me hope. I found hope that even though I may not be okay today, which is completely fine, that I might be better tomorrow, but I'd never know or come close to that feeling of serenity if I didn't find the strength to carry on today in order to see tomorrow.

My poem voices the fears and the anger society has tried to dismiss. Capturing the embodiment of all the corruption, repression, racism, ignorance, and lack of respect openly expressed in the world. The anger of being forced and chained to a society that I no longer believe in. The frustration of being controlled or the fear of a decision being made for me. The terror of losing or changing the essence of who I am to please or to find a place for myself in this society. The despair of never being able to break the cycle we call inequality or never being heard because of my minority. The exhaustion of putting in years of work to never be able to see a change. A fear of the uncontrollable, unpredictable aspects revolving around life.

This poem came about because I was tired of having to explain my pain to people who could never understand, who criticized my behavior and called it irrational, who've looked me in the eyes and claimed I was the problem all while I sat alone in the dark contemplating thoughts they'd never imagined. My poetry comes from wanting to understand the complexity of the world and turning around and trying to examine the way I see it functioning.

ABOUT SAMANTHA

Samantha James, a 20 year old student. Known as a self-assured and straightforward black woman. Constantly trying to display an open-minded attitude while embracing diversity. I'm the youngest daughter to two beautiful, first generation immigrant parents. Who throughout the years taught me the importance of being strong-willed and self-sufficient. I've been blessed with 2 older sisters and 4 amazing friends, who have allowed me to find joy in experiencing diverse elements of life. I'm an aunt to a very imaginative, energetic 6-year-old boy. I'm also a music enthusiast, self-taught poet, and an aspiring creative writer.

Instagram: @poetic_concept

ALLIE MAE BROSE

I sat on the shower floor, trying to process what just
    happened.
Letting the water pour over me like a blanket of comfort.
I sat there as the pain washed over me again.
This time in my thighs instead of my mind.

My eyes are focused on the new American flag on my
    pulsing thighs.
Red stripe after red stripe…
Blood pouring out like a battle field.
A battle between me and my mind.
My mind starts wondering,

"Look what YOU did"
"YOU are horrible"
"Why would YOU do this"

When all along it was my mind that did this.

I grasp the shower door in an effort to escape the blood
    and steam.
I throw on some pants in a desperate measure to cover
    up the pain I'm in.

"They won't understand"
"You promised not to do it again"

Anger starts to grab me, like a teenager holding on to
   their childhood for dear life.
Why did I do this to myself?

I force myself to come back to reality and think of
   ways to help myself…
I say…

Yes, today I cried….today I messed up,
BUT tomorrow I WILL RISE!
Tomorrow I WILL wear shorts
Tomorrow I WILL no longer be ashamed of myself
Tomorrow I WILL wear a real smile
Tomorrow I WILL look at myself in the mirror and
   love the reflection
Because I WILL RISE!
I have climbed the Mountain
Now it's time to descend down the other side.

BEHIND THE POEM

Hello this is Allie Mae. I wrote this poem because as a teenager in this day and age, balancing sports, work, and school can get a bit challenging. Not only is balancing those things tough, but I have had issues discussing my feelings when I begin to feel that overwhelming overload of stress. This is what led me to cutting.

Being stressed led to me trying to rely only on myself and not wanting to involve other people in my "drama." Feelings of guilt and anger kept me from talking to people who could have helped me. Once I started talking about the stress and emotions to someone trusted, I realized that communication helped release the pain without having to self harm.

Through this, I have begun to communicate my feelings, stress, and triggers to my parents and trusted friends and now no longer cut. I am not saying this has been a short and easy road, but it is possible, and I wish it for you. I hope that my writing will help you feel less alone and give the courage to speak out about your feelings and self harm. I hope you can learn to rise like I did.

ABOUT ALLIE MAE

Allie Mae Brose is a 17-year-old who loves family, friends, and her two dogs. She is a high school student who is on the girls wrestling team, and she also competes in Brazilian Jiu-jitsu.

Although she can be really hardcore on the mat, she is actually a sensitive, in-her-feels, caring teenager who enjoys loving and taking care of those around her. She also loves music, is in her high school elite choir, and enjoys playing the piano and ukulele. She hopes to one day become a teacher and an Olympic wrestler. She is just starting her writing journey, and this is her first piece to be shared with the world.

ASHON CALHOUN

Darkness waits at the horizon
Only held back by the sun
As the sun sags like the belt of Orion
The light then turns to run
Hot on its tail is the darkness
Ready to snuff out the light
Now that the sun is gone, it won't be long
Until it turns to night
Encased in a film of violet black
The world feels so dark
But never fear, hope is here
The light erupts from a spark

BEHIND THE POEM

When I wrote "Light and Dark," I was at a difficult point in my life. I had just returned from Army Basic Training and didn't have a solid home or job to return to. It was a scary situation for me. But I had faith that everything would be just fine. I wrote "Light and Dark" because I knew that no matter how dark this situation was, the light would always prevail. And it did. Every single time, the light erupted from a spark.

For what it's worth, we're too quick to seal our dreams in the dirt
We say the sky's the limit, yet we bury the sky in the earth
Come to terms, I know that reality burns
Awaiting to be great and then reality turns
The death of a dream that's what reality mourns
Despite mourning, in the morning, I'll believe my dreams again
No hocus pocus, no losing focus, only tunnel vision to the end
Whispers in my ear, killing a dream. I don't know what's expected
They kill a dream, and it's dead until I decide it's resurrected
I hope I don't choke and my dreams are not affected
But if I do lose hope I'll know it was by reasons that I suspected
Hard to believe, I've got dreams that are hard to achieve
Success does not come by rest, so it's hard to succeed
But I'm a dreamer

BEHIND THE POEM

When I wrote "Dreamer," I had been working various jobs. Each of them was more arduous than the last. Although I was thankful for my employment, I dreamed of work that did not require me to endure such demanding physical and mental stress. My dream was and still is to be a writer. I will see that dream achieved. At the time, however, I had low hopes. So I wrote "Dreamer" as a sort of pact with myself. A pact that I would continue to be a dreamer no matter how strenuous my situation was. These days, I have found new employment at a job that I love. However, I have not lost sight. I was and still am a dreamer.

ABOUT ASHON

Hello, my name is Ashon Calhoun. I'm 21 years old, and I'm from Pennsylvania. I have been writing poetry since I was 6 years old. I had my first poem published at 8. Ever since then, it has had such a major impact on my life. It's a way for me to tell a story of my emotions, situations, thoughts, etc. At first, it started as a hobby, but now being a writer has become my dream. I have recently been reciting my poetry at open mic events, and I love it. There's nothing like delivering your work to an audience. In short, poetry allows me to be a creator. Not just for others, but for myself.

Published works: WITS (Writers In The Schools), "The Canopy of Rhythm," "Outside Looking In," "A Walk on Our Wild Side."

Facebook: @CalTheCreat0r

Instagram: @cal_the_creator

TikTok: @cal_the_creator

VICKI
MANUEL

Fill me up Jesus
I'm running on empty..
I'm running to You Jesus...
Fill me up with..
Your love..
Your joy..
Your peace..
Your understanding..
Your gentleness...
not to much..
for its easier to fall when I am already down... this
world hurts Lord..
the hatred...
the anger..
the manipulation...
The sickness that plaques this world...
I've exhausted everything I have...
But You Lord, can fill me up..
Your peace overcomes..
Your love overpowers..
Your joy is contagious...
Your understanding opens my eyes..
Your gentleness opens my ears..
I'm running on empty..
I'm running on fumes..
I'm running to you..

BEHIND THE POEM

Learning to Lean on Jesus. This world tries to consume you, and the enemy tries to steal and destroy you, BUT Jesus heals you. Sometimes it is difficult to learn to depend on Jesus; our pride, our heartache, and lies we have been told can keep us from reaching out to HIM. The simplest thing is so hard sometimes.

In the last 4 years, I have had many difficult storms that left me empty. I cried many a tear. I was tired physically and emotionally, but thank God, each storm strengthened my faith and broke down my flesh so I could learn to lean on Jesus. That is exactly what He wants us to do. He wants to be our one and only. He wants us to have His eyes, His ears, His love, His knowledge, and His wisdom. No matter how difficult this world becomes, He is there to fill us up. God loves you, for He sent His only begotten Son. Jesus loves us so much that He died for us, rose, and now protects us. The only thing He asks us to do is believe in Him, to surrender to Him, to love Him, and to seek Him. He will do the rest.

My heart breaks...
My heart breaks, my eyes fill.
Knowing that you are hurting so; there isn't much I can do.
I can text you "hello" so you know I'm here; but your sorrow won't disappear.

You need time to understand that this storm shall come to an end.
The clouds will pass; you will soon feel the warmth of the sun kissing your face and joy will fill your heart.
You will look back and see this storm was a journey you had to take to get you where you are today.

My heart breaks, my eyes fill
knowing that you are hurting so..
Please remember that you are special in so many eyes.
You are a child of the one true King who is
guiding you toward the person you are meant to be.
While doors are closing others are opening; keep your eyes on the Lord for He he is leading you out of this storm...
My heart sings, my eyes fill knowing that you are with the one true King!!...

BEHIND THE POEM

Journey of Life. This life affects everyone. No one is exempt from hurt, pain, and turmoil, but no one is exempt from love, peace, and joy. Everyone has a story and a journey. It is often hard to watch someone go through a difficult time, but those difficult times are necessary to help them grow in Jesus. Jesus will always turn our mess into our message.

It is important to know when to step aside and when to help someone. Praying for them is always a must, and letting them know that you are there is a plus, but being an enabler is not. This is when we must trust in God, knowing that He has a plan for us. Knowing that He hears our prayers. When you are watching someone go through a rough time, keep your faith in Jesus, and lift that person up in your prayers; edify them to the Lord, and speak truth over them. Encourage them, worship with them, and let them know that the Lord loves them and that you love them.

ABOUT VICKI

Who is Vicki? Vicki is a Certified Christian Health Coach, a co-author, a wife, and most importantly, a Child of God.

Vicki is no different than you, a child of God who is learning to get through this journey of life. She is a new follower of Christ. As she learns from her experiences, she shares the knowledge and wisdom that God has given her to help others get through their experiences. She loves to help others reach their goals, to be there for their tears, to pray, to encourage, and to celebrate their victories.

CINDY
LESLIE

January twenty-ninth two-thousand and twenty
Could have been the end of me.
"Does she have a DNR?" they say.
I look at them and say, "today is not my day."
I feel no pain, but feel my strength ebb away.
I look in his eyes and see his fear.
"Don't worry," I say as I wipe away his tear.
Today is not my day.
Today we cry,
But tomorrow we will rise.
Fifteen days later I walked away.
VICTORY was proclaimed that day!
Today I can walk!
Today I can talk!
I am not a stroke survivor!
I am a stoke overcomer!
Today we rise!

BEHIND THE POEM

On the morning of January 29, 2020, I was getting ready for work as usual. It was a normal Wednesday morning, except it was just the 2nd morning of my new shift at DISH. I had to be at work at 8:00, so I had to leave my house at 7:45. At 7:00, I went to the bathroom to brush my teeth and finish getting ready. Then my life suddenly made a left turn. The next thing I knew I was sliding to the floor. Once on the floor, I was tired and decided to just lie there. My husband, Richard, heard the fall and came into the bathroom. There he found me on the floor, and of course, he was pretty scared.

After getting me up, he knew right away that something serious was wrong. I was able to help him find the number to call my work and let them know I would not be there. He put the phone on speaker. Chuck, the guy we were talking to, kept telling him it sounded like I had a stroke and that he should call 911 or get me to a hospital. I distinctly remember slurring, "I didn't have no stinkin' stroke." After all, old people have strokes, not young healthy people like me. I forget sometimes that I am not so young anymore. Turning 60 was quite a surprise to me.

After that point, I really don't remember much; All I know is what I have been told. Richard took me to the nearest ER, which was in Glenpool. After examining me, they told him I did not have a stroke, and he could take me home. I could answer all of their questions. *What is your name? Where are you? Who is the president?* This was during all the impeachment stuff, and I clearly remember answering that last one with, "well, Trump is, for today, but if the democrats get their way, maybe not tomorrow." I don't remember getting a CT scan, but they must have done one because they sent me a bill for it.

He let me sleep for a few hours, and when he woke me up, the left side of my face was a mess. A typical sign of stroke. He immediately called for an ambulance.

The paramedic was a guy that we knew back when he was just a kid. I love small town living and the connections you make. Darrell, the paramedic, confirmed that it was a stroke and advised we go to hospital by ambulance. Richard followed us there. I remember very little after leaving the first ER, but Richard has filled in the gaps.

The first real memory I have is of someone asking him if I had a DNR. I sat right up and assured them that I did not, and I expect them to keep me alive. After tests at St. John's, it appears that I had a stroke that morning, and sometime during the day at home I had a brain bleed. The next thing I remember was opening my eyes in the ICU and seeing the scared faces of my husband, my daughter, my granddaughter, my son, and my daughter- in-law. There was a neurosurgeon on call constantly during my 4 days in the ICU because my brain was swelling and it looked like I might need surgery to relieve it. I remember at one point, my daughter, Nicci, showed me a video of the ladies from her church having a prayer meeting. The ladies had someone standing in my place and laying hands on me through her. I know a lot of people were praying for me during this critical period, and God answered the prayers.

Many people came and went during my time in the ICU. That room was so full of love. The nurses were great and never ran anyone off, even though most of the time we were way over the number of allowed visitors. The swelling in my brain subsided, and I was released from the ICU and sent to the stroke unit, but not before being told that 1/3 of the right side of my brain was basically dead, and that it could be a long, hard recovery.

My first day in the stroke unit, I was walking in the hallway and working hard at getting my left hand to work properly. It did not want to cooperate. Three days later, I was released to go to a rehab center. My husband very seldom left my side. He spent every night sleeping in my room in some pretty uncomfortable places. Five days in rehab, and then we are headed home.

Don't get me wrong, recovery is a slow process. I wanted a microwave healing, but this was a crockpot healing. But a complete healing is coming. God continues to tell me to have peace with the process. In recent years, I had begun pulling away from God. I still loved Him, and knew He still loved me, but I was not truly serving Him. My stroke pulled me back in. I am ready to serve Him in any way he wants me to. I am getting stronger everyday. A special thanks goes to my granddaughter, Gracie Byrom, and my grandson, Daxton Leslie. Gracie kept me walking, and Daxton kept me moving. They both motivated me to keep moving forward and to keep fighting for my recovery. I know God is with me, and He is in control. "Those who wait upon the Lord will renew their strength they will soar on wings like eagles... They will run and not grow weary, they will walk and not grow faint." (Isaiah 40:31) I stand on this promise in God's word.

Keywords: wait upon the Lord. Crockpot, not microwave!

What I have learned during this period... my husband really does love me — and it is not just words; he has showed with actions. When we have a physical storm in life, the sun does not go away, we just can't see it through the clouds. During our life storms, the Son does not go away, sometimes we just can't see him through life's distractions. And God does heal, but often we have to have peace through a crockpot healing when what we want is that microwave healing. And he will work out everything for his glory if we just allow him too.

ABOUT CINDY

I have been married to the man God created just for me for 43 years. We live in Sapulpa, Oklahoma with our two fur babies and our chickens. I love spending time with my seven grandkids and my two great grandkids, playing in the garden, and taking road trips.

I have always enjoyed writing poetry, but have always kept it to myself. This is my first time to share my writing with the world.

Upcoming volume and special editions of
Today I Cried, but Tomorrow I'll Rise...

Volume 2 – *more poems on rising and overcoming,*
written by hearts from all over the world

Military edition – *the stories of our "Oscar Mikes"*
(An Oscar Mike is an injured veteran who chooses to rise
and overcome their new disability and inspire others to be
"on the move" to overcome and keep living.)

Fighting the Addiction edition – *the stories of addicts who*
are rising, overcoming, and inspiring others to keep the fight

If you would like to take the opportunity to be part
of any of these editions or volumes, share your story,
and bring hope and inspiration to many, please
email Nicci Jo at niccijowrites@gmail.com.